THIS IS FOR THE
WOMEN
WHO
DON'T
GIVE A
FUCK

A COLLECTION OF POEMS BY
JANNE ROBINSON

Copyright © 2017 by Janne Robinson.

This book was designed by KJ Parish and published by Thought Catalog Books, a publishing house owned by The Thought & Expression Company. It was printed in the United States and was published in an edition of 3,000 copies.

ISBN 978-1-945796-41-8

"Women love, love—not men."

—Luca Villani

"Women like Janne are more than important, they are vital to the fabric of this society. She exudes strength and grace in a combination like few I've ever known and her words are reminders, often fierce, often gentle, to that deep well of power inside her. As long as she writes, I'll read."

—*Tyler Knott Gregson*

"In a consumer society we are starving for the real and authentic. Janne's words nourish that craving. If that which is spoken from the heart is sacred, these poems are like prayers."

—*Dianne Whelan*

"When Janne has a new poem written, I shut my life down to do nothing but read it, and then when I turn my life back on, everything is better."

—*James Altucher*

"This world needs Janne. She is a force of nature. Her authenticity, drive and vulnerability are giving people permission everywhere to access their truth and their greatness. She is a new voice of consciousness and a breath of fresh air."

—*Kyle Cease*

"It is rare to meet anyone who makes revolution nature."

—*Alan Clements*

"When Janne appears, she has that rare ability to light up the room, and sometimes the mountain or the entire forest! Read with her and be transported to the loving, kind, fantastic and thoughtful world we all want to believe exists. I do."

—*Peter Tunney*

"Janne personifies courage of self-expression. She is a beacon of light and an inspiration in self-worth and leading by example."

—*Austin Bisnow*

"Janne 'gives a fuck' about what it means to live—to truly live—in the rawness of this human experience, in the fullness of our potential and to the truest beat of the unchained heart. Her words wake you up, rattle your chains and beckon you to live and love with the fierceness of a soul who doesn't give a fuck about the fears holding back your truth. In her poems we pick up the lost tracks of our soul's frontier."

—*Nicole Davis*

"Fearless inspiration to peel back layers of herself and the world along the way, Janne has an uncanny ability to offer a lens into the human experience in the ever-changing modern world. Poetry to find strength and cut through the confusion. Janne's voice is bold, compassionate and commanding. Women are the future."

—*Peter Goetz*

"I'm drawn to truth tellers. To people who dive below the surface and tell me what's real. The people who express their souls and make me a little more in touch with mine. When I read Janne's words I feel like I'm mainlining passion and on a superhighway to my heart. There's no greater gift than this."

—*Mark Groves*

"The world has been graced with some powerful women: the scientist Rosalind Franklin, anti-slavery advocate Harriet Beecher Stowe, Emmeline Pankhurst who led the women's right to vote movement, Anne Frank, and so many more. The 21st century has Janne Robinson. She successfully colours outside the lines in a way that is not only provocative, but is sometimes messy, and always engaging. Her honesty, vulnerability and directness inspire women all over the globe. 100 years from now women all over the world will remember her name."

—*Rae-ann Wood-Schatz*

Daniel Kingsbury—you will live etched in my brain with your broad shoulders amongst the yellow bloom of Broome the first week of June. And when the yellow has fallen to the earth—you will live on through the limbs and lips and heart born in these poems. Your love gave the wounded parts of me wings that did not know they were meant to fly.

One of the greatest gifts of my life will forever be being loved by you.

A book dedication is a small offering to the man who loved me with the love I denied myself my whole life—I hope they have libraries in heaven.

THERE'S COBWEBS ON HER VAGINA

the gynecologist replies

removing his head from between her freckled thighs

her mother chokes on the air

p-pardon?

It's from a society that shames women for enjoying sex

one that puts purity rings on their fingers

promises them away to God

away from pleasure

pleasure is shameful

you hear?

God is the only one that loves you

What if the husband is a jackrabbit?

what if he lacks all there is to know about making a
woman moan?

what if she dies not having her soul ripple?

her body shake

fall apart

from the hands and tongue of a man who has done his work

a lover of all things woman

God, what if he's gay?

what if he wishes to be making love to a man?

heaven forbid her body is never touched with the tenderness

that we deserve from the moment we are born

It's from a society that throws half-naked sexualized women
in sunglasses commercials making us hide our daughters' eyes

while the men smoking Cuban cigars laugh

making millions off the easiest marketing idea invented

the female body is the greatest piece of art

of course it sells

Shame on us for giving it away

then playing the victims

the big bad media wolves

forcing our hands to paper to sign

there are no victims here

women, are to blame

It's from a society that shrieks at nipples

turns away

they're the same as mine

but

but

they're sexual!

Put them away

I can feel the breeze on my sweltering chest in August

but

you

must

cover

yours

It's from a society that cuts off women's genitals

doesn't give them the right to vote

to work

to live

to love who they choose

covers them in clothes

no, not to hide them from the sun

Marries them away at fourteen

to a twenty-one-year-old called Jose

who drinks four bottles of whisky a day

who falls asleep drunk after they have sex each night

boring

missionary sex

with no foreplay

while she speaks quietly into the night of wanting to be
a lawyer

of how she would bring justice with all her might

He closes her legs

the mother's mouth is still dropped

masturbation, 2 times a day—3 if needed

his white coat wisps behind him as the door shuts

Oh mamma

the world we live in is changing.

THESE ARE THE LOVE STORIES
I'LL NEVER HAVE

The floors shake as the city tram

flies by

I wish it were the hardwood floors shaking as your feet
moved six feet from your closed door to mine

I wish you would hover to knock

go to leave

and then stay

decide to know

and risk

and I would wake up and sit in the big windows that look
upon a city of strangers and yellow taxicabs

and you could hit the white of your cigarette into an empty
beer bottle

and I would read to you

slowly

and deliberately

past when the stars have gone to bed

This would be better than the dream I had

and the dreams I won't have

for if I move my foot two inches

I can know what it would feel like

for a moment

to touch you

and if I touch you I can know if I someday wish to lie
nose to nose

on white pillows

and drift my fingers upon a back

that has never felt these lips

but instead you say goodnight darlin'

in a drawl that's been practiced to steal the knees of women
who want to be stolen and we go to sleep.

I WOKE UP TODAY AND DIDN'T MISS YOU ANYMORE

do you know what that feels like?

rain after weeks of being thirsty

food after days of being hungry

waking up to hear the piano one morning, after a lifetime of being deaf

water, after wandering parched and delirious through the desert for days

air after holding my breath for weeks

opening my eyes, after existing in the dark

speaking, after living in silence

taking bricks off bones that didn't know they were holding a weight that wasn't theirs

I have a power in my belly, a heat in my bones and my heart is clear

I'm back

my heart is alive.

I SOMETIMES LET THE KETTLE HOWL TOO LONG

I hear it, see it in the corner of my eye

I let it be

singing quietly into the night

it can wait

this world needs to learn to wait

wait for a love worth having

company worth keeping

a job worth working

its call is comforting

like the sound of the furnace beginning to roar

in the dead of a cold night

a candle burning in broad daylight

red flannel on a rainy summer night

a song I love playing whimsically in a café I don't know

making it feel more familiar

more at home

comfort has its place in this world

mine is in the green kettle

with a steel handle that burns

demanding patience and respect.

I SHOULD GET A JOB

I can't afford all this

this log palace

this gluten-free cereal that costs eight dollars a box

what starving artist can afford cereal that costs eight dollars
a box?

I'll get a job when the words stop I say

but they don't stop

every time I have time to pick up a pen

or a keyboard

they come

they harass me

when I seek rest

when I seek food

in conversations

making me leave abruptly

so I can scramble for ink and space

pour it out

scribble it down alone

I just want to sit in my captain's chair

with the broken arm I meant to fix

but live with

at dusk and dawn

(when I am awake for dawn)

watch the fields below my cabin light on fire

purple armies of petals

I want to throw my heart at the world

at sunshine

trees

strangers

have room to catch it when it flies back

words are in the rustle of trees

in that piece of wood

there

in the man who I sat on a log and passed the day with today

they are in the hellos with the hummingbird as it zooms by my balcony each morning

no, words are my job

I guess I'll have to start eating cheaper cereal.

LET THERE BE WORDS, HE PRAYS

I always know a man isn't good for me
if there's no poems
I once lived with a man for six days
and the words didn't come
they stopped
there was silence on paper
and not a welcome silence
like when you turn a fan off
that's been buzzing for four hours
taking up space unknowingly in your ear's brain

When you are making love to a poet
there should never be a word desert
my pen was parched of ink
I pulled my hair
the love wasn't there
and then I left him

I place my cup down on the wooden table
I see the sweat trickle
on my maybe lover's forehead
let there be words
he prays.

FUCK PENSIONS

I used to say that I didn't value money
I always had it, spent it, made rent without a sweat
I paid the bill, chose the nicest red by the glass
they knew my first name at my favorite stores
we both knew they liked my credit card
but it's nice when they know you

Now
I am grateful for every dime in my car change tray
I am grateful for every morsel of food on my plate
I eat it all
I am grateful when I have enough money to buy propane
to have a hot shower at my cabin

The other day I had 60 bucks to last me three days
I bought groceries
opted out of a shower
fought with a Coleman stove from the sixties for 45 minutes
on my deck in hopes of a coffee
it won
but when I had a coffee two days later—I won

I'm a cushioned and privileged broke
I know my mother won't let me starve
I'm also too proud to ask for help
just yet

I'd rather eat oats and deli meat

remind myself what it takes

being broke is okay

there are some of us who have big houses that are empty

fancy cars

with seats where love has never been made

shirts without wrinkles

china in cabinets

that have never been eaten on

nice whisky with no company worth having

to share it with

record collections of a king

listened to alone

Why?

because they've worked their life away

and for what?

a pension? early retirement? so your father smugly approves?

fuck his approval

work to work to work to die

these people are the real peasants

I'll take freedom over a pension any day

where are my stocks?

remove the 'T'

and then you'll find them in the first drawer

Where are my investments?

in this leather-bound notebook

in this prolific soul

in that man's smile

my freedom lies here

with my broke ass

sleeping in my car by the ocean

showering in salt for two days

because my only source of income is renting my own bed
out for a night

it's worth it

look at this view!

I'm young

I can afford to have an aching back from sleeping in a car

keep your pension

these experiences make me rich.

CONVERSATIONS WITH GRIEF

Knock knock

who is it?

I yell from beneath the bubbles of the bath

oh, hey Grief

you asshole

come on in

I pour two glasses of whisky in tall drams

don't add ice as ice is for assholes who don't know that scotch is whisky

why don't we invite God, while we're at it?

hey!

God!

you big jackass

why don't you come down and explain to me this cruel joke?

explain to me why at 10:44 PM

I am hit like sunlight in the face after a night of drinking

by loss

of an eternal heartache

explain to me why you didn't make a fucking undo button?

I take a drag of a cigarette I would never smoke

the yellow burn

chugging like a train that has lost its drive to live

I hit the white into an ashtray

Grief!

you still there, pal?

how fucking long does this take?

almost three months and I'm brought back to zero daily

can you prescribe me a new heart?

What's your big plan, God?

what do you do with those of us left standing?

don't tell me we're all one

don't tell me to feel him in the goddamn breeze

I'm done eating the esoteric bullshit

just look me in the eye and tell me why he's gone

Silence?

big surprise

the two heroes have nothing to say

I laugh a mad laugh

clapping echoes off the white tiles

both of you get the fuck out of my bathroom and leave
me alone.

OH, YOU'RE A WRITER?
so you drink too much coffee
stay up all night
drinking whisky
swearing at the world
with your pen?
basically, yes
so, you're a human?
you eat, drink, breathe, sleep, shit
graduate, go to college
wear a tie, sit at a desk
work for your parents
think the world's about "who you know"
something about a blood diamond
and an I do
suburbia, procreate, cars, fence, pets
9–5, laundry
vacation because you're burnt out or bored
I can do that too
I write because I am desperate to be anything but you.

WE ARE A SOCIETY WITH A
HARD-ON FOR THINGS

Things, things, things
we are a society with such a hard-on for things
just go

Go

Go do the things you love
travel to the places you wish to breathe the air
stop waiting for life to hold your hand
stop waiting 'til you have your shit together
having our shit together is a myth
for even when we are standing still the earth is moving
it's impossible to keep up with ourselves
the moon is full
the sky is orange
the Ylang Ylang blossoms are in bloom today
not tomorrow
the only word worth saying today is

Go.

THIS IS FOR THE WOMEN WHO DON'T GIVE A FUCK

The women who are first to get naked, howl at the moon and jump into the sea.

The women who drink too much whisky, stay up too late and have sex like they mean it.

The women who know they aren't sluts because they enjoy sex, but human beings with a healthy sexual appetite.

The women who will ask you for what they need in bed.

This is for the women who seek relentless joy; the ones who know how to laugh with their whole souls.

The women who speak to strangers because they have no fear in their hearts.

The ones who wear "night makeup" in the morning or don't own mascara.

The women who know their worth, plant their feet and roar in their brilliance.

The women who aren't afraid to tell a man to get the fuck out of her heart if he doesn't honor her worth.

This is for the women who rock combat boots with frilly skirts.

The women who swear like truck drivers.

The women who hold the people who wrong or harass them with fierce accountability.

The women who flip gender norms and false limitations

the bird and live to run successful companies giving "the man" a run for his name.

The ones who don't find their success a compliment just because they have a vagina.

Women like Gloria Steinem who, when she was told, "We want a writer, not a woman. Go home," kept writing anyway.

This is for the women who drink coffee at midnight and wine in the morning, and dare you to question it.

For the women who open doors for men and are confident enough to have doors opened for them.

Who use "no" to be in service for themselves.

Who don't give a damn about pleasing the world, and do sweetly as they wish.

For the superheroes—the single moms who work three jobs to make it. I salute your resilient, cape-flapping, ambitious selves.

This is for the women who throw down what they love, and don't waste time following society's pressures to exist behind a white picket fence.

The women who create wildly, unbalanced, ferociously and in a blur at times.

The women who know love is not about gender and love who they wish.

The women who know how to be busy and know how to plant their feet in the earth and get grounded.

These are the women I want around me.

MAMMA DIDN'T RAISE NO FUCKING PRINCESS

Don't go in there!
why?
there's some pee on the floor?
the toilet seat's never been cleaned?
I'll have to hover and squat and not touch the walls
for shit's been smeared upon them?
mamma didn't raise no fucking princess
toilet paper's for the rich
just give it a shake
and wash in the shower later
the people here sleep on wooden slats
they have saunas and sweat the dirt out
instead of showers
their bodies know not of hot water
they cannot complain about lumpy pillows
sagging mattresses
for they sleep on slats where the cold seeps in and stays 'til
the morning
they wipe their eyes for dirt
and the thirteen-year-old daughter works 10-hour days
for $80 a month
black hands from polishing shoes under the yellow sun
because her father's an alcoholic
and her mother can't support four children

so no, I won't piss in the privileged toilets

I'll squat a little

so I can remember what I have and where I could've come from

getting dirty in doses

does mounds for our humility.

People ask me what it was like

being raised

by two gay moms

I tell them

my wallet is a little bit lighter

on mother's day

and a little bit heavier on father's day.

I'M THE WORST WRITER ON THE PLANET

what kind of writer doesn't carry a fucking pen?

a notepad?

I walk down the Grey Nuns hospital

bleak buzzing lights

backless blue hospital dress

beneath this coat you can see my ass!

I want to shout

I'm having more fun than you—I'm naked

I smirk

well, naked with socks

floundering for a pen

drug rep posters splattered on the walls

"She's smiling, but what she doesn't know...is that she has HPV!"

dickheads

inducing fear

selling unnecessary drugs

news, hospitals—all pushing fear

tired nurses

mundane lives

they shit on my ears

not enough rooms, too many patients

they are tired, overworked

talking about shitty lives

shitty husbands, shitty boyfriends

boring, dull, pointless

get me out of here

I look at my feet

I fainted in this chair

"Are you pregnant?"

I have a flash

uneasy

no

but yes before

fuck off

and fuck off with your $100

3-step shots

"It's mandatory for all grade fives now, you know?"

if we all thought for ourselves

we'd say no in grade five

we would say, "Fuck the juice box—you're not putting that in my arm."

in Guatemala kids in grade five take care of their entire families

North American children have all the resources

and no responsibility

no gratitude

no understanding

we just shit away our privilege

wasting our brains on video games

"Doctor is just changing—he had a messy appointment."

what the fuck does that mean?

vaginal juices? breast pumps?

glorified gynecologist nay more

"Jane"

her smile's fake

she hates her job

that's not my goddamn name

legs on stirrups

open wide, edge closer

I wish I shaved my legs

"Oh, that's by Bowen Island. I hear there's a lot of gay people out there."

there are gay people everywhere

asswipe

there are also straight people everywhere

you don't ever say, "Oh, Boston—I hear there's a lot of straight people who golf there!"

do you?

I hate hospitals.

EVERYONE'S A FUCKING BLOGGER

Every Dick Jane Harry is a writer

every jackass with a typewriter app is a poet

every thirteen-year-old who has an iPhone is a photographer

every thirty-year-old white woman has quit her job to become a yoga teacher

every esoteric asshole is doing ayahuasca in Colombia

every feather wearing hippie knows how to do reiki

every ad on my Facebook is how to triple your money to become a coach

starting your own podcast show?

original

no one is doing that

lululemon is mandatory for yoga and gluten-free is the new Friday

while you're at it come to my goddess ceremony where women drink cacao tea

we are the esoteric millennials who wash our face with Eckhart Tolle

brush our teeth with Rumi

and wipe our ass with Paulo Coelho

we say namaste without knowing what it means

follow teachers without knowing why they're on a pedestal in the first place

go to self-growth weekends where everyone is enlightened during the day

and does drugs and fucks each other at night

where founders and coaches try to sleep with their clients
where we slap shaman on a business card
and have no problem sleeping at night.

There is dirt and dust and wet jean shorts from waterfalls and sunshine and a day lived hard. We rip, chasing the last of the day frantically. There is a bottle of merlot, it's open and untouched.

We could miss the sunset, it happens every day. But we could also chase it, and I'm here to chase magic. I'm here to take the last slice of red hot sun as it sinks into la mer and the white wisps of waves—mimicking the clouds above.

We throw shoes, a torn and tattered and rusty stained blue blanket, and rush to feel the ocean with our toes. We made the show. And we leave our cell phones and cameras, away, in our bags.

There is gooey melted ice cream on my leg, salt on my face and sunshine in my hair.

It is unspoken that this is a moment to be devoured without distraction—to become a vivid, lit-on-fire memory we can taste and smell and see and feel years from now because we are showing up, dropped on our knees with gratitude to be present.

To be alive is such a rich thing. To have legs to stand upon and tear into this world with our wide open red beating hearts.

The sky is orange and purple, Venus shines—there, trying to steal the show but it can't, for if the clouds were a woman, she would be so beautiful the orchestra would drop their harps, their strings, their drums—they would weep and look away and look back and lust and love and fall away.

And all of a sudden my isolationist heart is hit so terrifyingly hard in my chest—I don't want to be alone.

I want souls who I can fall in love with in forty-eight hours. Souls who rock their bliss hard. The decadent connections I stumble upon, and moments like this remind me of the beauty of being together.

Let's chase magic and write poetry, fall asleep together in hammocks, flirt with love, or perhaps loving love and get old and wrinkly and do it all over again tomorrow.

Dear yesterday, I love you.

Dear tomorrow, you better be goddamn beautiful—I've got expectations lit on fire.

HELP, I'M MAKING LOVE TO AN ITALIAN

Help!
I'm making love to an Italian
he has brown eyes like honey
blond hair that's a mess
he makes me rich dark espresso
plays my legs like a harp
cooks breakfast to Yiánnis Chryssomállis
as I lie half asleep in blue sheets

Help!
I'm making love to an Italian
he spends eight hours making lasagna
thinks in Spanish
holds me
strongly
although I object to cuddling while I sleep
he holds me anyway
and I let him

Help!
I'm making love to an Italian
he's boisterous and loud
yet patient and loving
he drags me home

pulls me from the middle of the street where I lay drunk
off wine and stars

walks me home

when he'd rather be asleep.

WE NEED LESS DICKHEADS AND MORE PEOPLE LIVING LIKE THEY MEAN IT

Sleep 8 hours a night

drink twelve cups of water

drink milk

eat meat or you'll waste away

like those grass-eating fucks

the ones who won't eat gummy bears

because they contain honey

and the bees had to work

God save the bees!

doing their jobs on this planet

like everyone else

bee cruelty—you're an idiot

I'll eat those

they're delicious

I'm deliriously happy

haven't slept enough

drank three times my weight in coffee

no milk

it's all crap—marketing cheerleaders for dairy did their jobs well

all I need is coffee, connection and ink

I'm fed

I'm the happiest fucker in this airport

moping around because you had to wait a second in line

it's life!

you must wait

you instant gratification shitheads

if you don't want to be here

go home

what's at home? your TV?

your Steve Jobs gadgets?

that's what you're in a rush for?

to get off the plane and turn your phone on

idiot

life is precious

you're wasting all our time with your melodramatic sighs

because the woman forgot to take her belt off

Jesus

there are worse things

we are so lucky

I want to drop ungrateful fucks

in places of conflict

you complain about a baby crying on an airplane

it's an inconvenience, isn't it?

try dodging bullets

watching vultures eating the bodies of those who didn't make it

while you complain about your leg room

someone is bed-ridden with disease

without the means to buy medicine

do you know how lucky you are?

has your soul quit seeing gratitude?

quit complaining

exist differently

we need less dickheads and more people living like they mean it.

I AM NOT HERE TO FIX YOU

I am not here to entertain you

I am not here to fix you

I am not here to rescue, heal or revive you

I am not here to be talked at

I am not here to give you all my energy

I am not here to make your story my own

I am not here to just listen

I am not here to make you whole

I am not here to make you happy

I am not here to make it all dissipate

I am not here to distract you from the tedious and mundane

I am not here to mask your sadness and feed your insecure heart

I am not here to hold your hand

I am not here to be a band aid

I am not here to give you all of me

I am here to love you strongly

I am here to love you equally

I am here to be an addition to the joy you already have

I am here to rest in, but not collapse into

I am here to support you, hear you, see you

I am here to make love to you

I am here to love you sweetly and gently and ferociously with all my might.

I'M GOING TO WRITE POEMS ABOUT YOU
it is a statement dressed up in an almost question
he rolls his cigarette paper
the fan blows hot air
he doesn't object

This is a disclaimer
if you make love to a writer's heart
you're bound to wind up inside the pages
even if he objected
it wouldn't matter
he knows this
perhaps it's why he sits in silence.

HOW TO CATCH A WOMAN

by the throat

he says

with strong dark Italian espresso

with pasta

and love

and you must make the food with love

and it sounds like shit, cliché

but is true!

and then, sex

love twice

over again

'til the soul is folded

my eyes laugh

for I know it is true.

I EAT MUSICIANS LIKE YOU FOR BREAKFAST

What are you doing later?

not rolling around in your sweet honey, little bee

I eat musicians like you for breakfast

I know this dance

backstage access

dick access too

but not heart access

no that takes more than flirting

underneath a hot pink sky

candle lanterns

stars abloom

that would take love

and time

and you leave to wherever have you

at 3 PM tomorrow

so run along

try your long brown hair

hazel eyes

on another girl

one who doesn't know electric guitars are penis extensions

who will fall into white sheets

slept in by many

loved by none.

I JUST WANT TO WAKE UP AND SHOUT I LOVE YOU'S AT EACH OTHER

not really yelling

(until we have coffee)

but the I love you's in each touch along our spines

in each kiss along your neck

in the way we wake up and feel so goddamn blessed to have found each other in this bat shit crazy world and get to maneuver through it together

in the way we don't take any of this—for granted

in a way that makes our love insurmountable and unstoppable

that scoffs at distance, for we know the importance of space within our togetherness[1]

you do not complete me, nor I you

we were full before

grounded

before

and that's why when we dance we have so much fun

a love that is so strong, that we replace jealousy with the confidence that we are such delectable lovers the whole world wants a piece

and that at the end of the day all we really have is the choice to choose each other

to wake up each day and say, "I choose you. I want you."

and hope like a motherfucker we're both up to our necks in the same kind of love

and then do it all over again the next day.

---

1   *Gibran, Kahlil, The Prophet, Alfred A. Knopf, 1923*

RUBIA

Blue sheets torn

escaping the mattress

rich red cherry wood creaks

brown and blue tapestry hangs gently

plays with the wind

burning infancy

he reads

blond hair pulled back

hazel eyes

black coffee in hand

rubia he calls

I wish to connect the brown freckles

moles on your back like constellations with my fingertips
my lips

sit for hours with you as a canvas

between these legs

paint and paint upon you

Soft kisses drift upon my spine

upon the arches of my legs, my hips

my feet

my back

he hasn't even made me lasagna yet.

THIS WAS WRITTEN AFTER A SUICIDE

It's funny

one person throws in the cards to the deck

and it's 10:49 PM on a Friday

and part of me could throw in the cards

too

and I stand in the white light

as the fridge buzzes

drinking milk out of the carton

and wonder how many other people left behind in grief

consider death as a vice

I'll continue watching crap TV

and pretend I didn't have that thought

because I want to keep on living

but the thought is there

you know

and I'll just say it

in case the rest of you were thinking it too.

FACEBOOK

I pull up the white screen

it shocks my eyes

they yell a little

what the fuck are you looking in there for?

it's none of your business

you are just eyes

you are only here to see

so I look

there is nothing there

there is no love

there is no affection

it's just a buzzing, bleak screen full of nothing

it can't hold me in the blackest of the night

yet we live here

you and I

we think it's real

like a dollhouse with mini tables

chairs

shoes

beds

we eat, sleep, and love on Facebook

neglecting our others in the daylight

what the fuck are you doing in here?

the screen says

hike a mountain

drink the clouds

make love to tender thighs

put buttercups in your hair

draw a map of your own star constellations

no!

I yell grouchily

there's something in here

I'm sure

sometimes I feel it

it coats the loneliness for a little while

like a red pill after a bottle of Ardbeg whisky

like being loved after chasing the loveless

and we sit up all night

scrolling like zombies

waiting for our screens to give us what we need

and they never will

and we'll never leave.

FUCK BUCKET LISTS

fuck figuring it all out and having our shit together before we land our penguin

carve a pebble out of whatever you have

it'll do

better yet, be your own goddamn penguin

we are constantly trying to be so together

make x amount of money, live in x neighborhood, drive x car, be x weight

after I've made X I'll meet Z

be your own Z!

live vicariously through yourself

no one is good enough to do the things you wish to do, other than you.

LISTEN UP YOU BIG BOYS

the old boys' club no longer belongs in shop culture

take your sexism

your chauvinism

your homophobia

your alpha testosterone

your racism

your porn

your harassment

your sabotage

your alienation

your ostracization

your threats

your pack mentality

your sexual jokes about me eating a banana

home

show up with your wrenches

like the rest of us

and do your fucking job

what about the ones who won't listen?

the old boys who laugh at feminism?

the men who don't take equality seriously?

some of them will never change

some of them will just die as dicks

but some of us are willing to change

and that's why we stand up to speak.

YOUR WORDS ARE NO GOOD TONIGHT

You like classical music?

he says with a slip of a smile

that mocks playfully

he looks around for my brown loafers and reading glasses

yes

I reply

not moving an inch

there's too many words in this world

in my head

in my heart

on the streets

on the telephone

in the coffee shops

and the restaurants

and the mechanic garages

everywhere I go there are words

and sometimes it feels so good to turn them off

to let strings dance

trumpets sing

cellos groan

violins speak

my brain needs classical music like my lungs need air

now fetch me Brahms or Beethoven or Vivaldi

and touch me only with the words of your lips
and the syllables of your thumbs
your words are no good tonight.

I'M NOT AFRAID TO TELL YOU

that I am beautiful
for being at home in my heart
and heart's shoes
did not come to me at birth

I've unravelled, searched
done copious amounts of work
I've travelled and done
seen and asked
participated in this planet
my growth
I've sat with my shadow
soul spelunked

The beauty that we hear of
cannot always be seen
but it can be felt
in the eyes of the ones
that shout sunshine
the ones with no fear in their hearts
that aren't threatened by
the brilliant existence
the magnificence of the others
that roam beside us

Beauty is seeing that woman
there

saluting her
in her exquisiteness
knowing we see that brilliance
because we, too
are at home in our
whole souls
bodies, too

So if this is vain
I am vain
if this is narcissistic
I am a narcissist

I would rather be
all of these things
than shake
with fear in my heart
whenever a beautiful woman
walks into a room

So I will say it
again
now
listen with softer ears
I
am
beautiful.

We collapse

taking each other's bodies

for hours

the bottle of red

there

is half empty

I pull you in and taste spice

the cabin is full of sweat

heat

from limbs and hearts

sweet moans blend with the rushing of the creek

falling of the rain

we've made love

here and there

in circles, on that chair

those stairs

come here

falling into a bed naked of sheets

pulling each other back down for air

over and over

should we get sheets?

fuck the sheets

I'll lie anywhere with you

just keep touching me with those hands

that mouth

the daylight breaks

does having sex count as sleeping?

I take you again

your body ripples

trembles

falls apart beneath me.

I AM NOT MY SADNESS

I am not my joy

I am not my jealousy

I am not my head held high

I am not my insecurity

I am not guilt

nor am I my anger

these emotions are visitors

to the vessel that I am

and I love them

and feel them

and don't attach stories to them

or identify with them

they simply come to sit on my stoop

I drink tea with Anger

and I hear her rage

I see her flex her biceps and her blood boil

I see her face popping and arms swinging

I invite Sadness to sit beside me

she is blue

everything she touches turns blue

I see the weight of her heart as the words fall slowly out
in tears

and then I kiss her goodnight

Joy is next

and she is standing and talking quite loudly with her hands as she tells a grandiose story with gleaming eyes and laughter shaking the mountains around me

she is light and I feel relief at her presence

she is like sunshine and strawberries picked from the baseball field on a Sunday behind my grandmother's house

eaten with dirty hands

And then Guilt shows up

dragging his feet as he comes to lean beside me on the white post

and the weight of his existence oozes and draws the energy from the earth

he is born with a heaviness he does not know how to shake and I do not try explain or heal or fix him

I just let him stand beside me as the sun goes down

drinking the glumness that he is prescribing

Jealousy shows up before I've had coffee

she is wearing leather pants and she hisses at the world while she sways her hips

holding a cigarette between her red lips she seethes and spits

she is fire

Soon after is her sister in crime Insecurity

Insecurity walks tentatively up the steps

she's not sure if she's welcome

even after I've welcomed her in

she doesn't want to sit

for she is so afraid of taking up space

and so I let her shake beside me

I just love her like that

And then Arrogance rolls up

in a Mercedes-Benz

he revs his engine with the tenacity of a child longing to be seen

and instead of rolling my eyes and telling him he misses the love of his mother he never received

and that her love isn't out here in this world

that he won't get it

like that

with his loud car

it's inside

and he must sit still to find it

I see him

I smile

I welcome his loudness

his boisterous presence into my arms

I take his broad shoulders and stiff neck reaching for the stars

into my heart

You see

you and I

are not our emotions

they are visitors

passing in the day and in the night

And all you must do

when they come knocking

is welcome them inside

with the knowingness that they truly never stay forever if
you just honor and feel them with presence

and love them through.

THE DARK SIDE OF PARADISE

Palm trees
brown warm skin
red hot sunsets that kiss the bottom of the sea
pura vida
pura vida
except
don't you dare go to the beach at night
because there are dozens of nameless women
raped in between the trunks of the palm trees

One man held down
by two men
while his girlfriend was raped before his eyes
they were just walking back from dancing
wanted to watch the white moon
in paradise
it was dealt with
not by the police
but by the two men who held down the rapist and drowned him
the next week

I am not sad he drank foam
instead of air

It's paradise
except for the hotel with the large lizard

white dirty walls

window curtains stained with dust

I never liked the energy in there

steered clear

found out the owner was found dead

feet sticking out of a washing machine

It's paradise

except for those three women on their quad who got mugged and raped by the river filled with crocodiles

in broad daylight

did you hear their screams?

It's paradise

except for those young kids who get hopped up on cocaine and pull women off the dance floor at the full moon parties

or when they go to the bathroom

and take their turn inside of her

while the techno screams

It's paradise

except for the young girl

who a man tried to lure into the bushes

while I surfed with her dad in the sea

she got out

but whose daughter didn't?

It's paradise except for those women who are too afraid
to hold the men accountable
because this isn't the USA
and the cops will ask you
what were you wearing?

I am mad at them
anyway
for leaving
on big jet planes
letting rapists roam free in the sunshine
leering and waiting

It's paradise except for that morning I was checking the
surf at 5 AM
and an Argentinian ran by me screaming
there's a man with a gun
there's a man with a gun
go back to your house
close your windows

It's paradise except when you get chased out of town
shot and bleed dry in the streets

I love it here
except when I feel the screams
muffled by the hands of men
as their entitled dicks

ram in and out

of a vagina

that they claimed

unasked

and then can walk into a café in broad daylight the next day

while people only whisper rapist

and give him his change

If you want to make a crime against the government

I don't give a fuck

Rob a bank?

it's money

I don't give a fuck

But if you sell a woman's body on the market

mug a child and drug her

keep her in a room

where men in old blue t-shirts

pay $5 to fuck her

before she's hit puberty

If you rape

and take

the body of a woman

that is not yours

I give a fuck

Rape is unforgivable
in my eyes

My mamma said if anyone ever raped me
she would kill them
even if it meant going to jail for the rest of her life
and my soul agrees
if you take the flesh of a woman that is not yours
may you burn in the red-hot coals of a hell I don't believe in.

Zizikas

my father says

as the deafening roar of a million insects takes over my ears

They only live for a few weeks

so they are talking all the time

they have to say everything

before they die.

I WILL NOT WAIT TO DIE TO BEGIN TO LIVE

What are you doing right now?

Go outside

Go

Go stand in the goddamn sunshine

smile at someone

see the people around you

see the pink flowers that hang heavy

the red poppies that reach for the heavens

feel the air in your lungs and be grateful they rise and fall on their own

that your heart is beating strongly in your chest without assistance

call the people you love, hell, get in a car and drive to their doorstep and remind them how much you love them

we are not here to waste time not living, breathing, moving, loving

we are not just here to work, eat, shit, sleep, make money, spend money—we are here to love

please go outside right now and look at the mountains

use your phone to extend some love instead of emails

it's not a request today—it's a plea

do not wait to die, to begin to live.

"Why do you love her?" they ask

"She's like sunshine," I say

sunshine that blasts through the rain

as it collects in between the cobblestone streets at dusk

where the pink flowers hang richly in the orange light

their bleeding hearts

unable to raise their faces to the sun.

CHARLIE

A haze of tired faces

ten hours spent in traffic jams

Jesus, give us a break

the 'stache of a '70s porn star

shirt unbuttoned

gold rimmed glasses

bronzed chest

a triangle on his left arm

the eight-pack only twenty-something-year-olds have

goddamn I'm not done loving hot twenty-something-year-olds with butts of steel from surfing

I'll grow old and date old men eventually

there he is

in between the sea of blues and reds

Waldo at the end of a 24-hour flight

cold airplanes and hot buses

we drink a bottle of $6 rum

what else is there to do?

take kisses that would taste like salt

if we could touch it with our feet

I like your poems

he says

good, you'll likely be in one

quit your job tomorrow

pack up and leave

come be with me

there's hope in my heart

there's always hope when there's a man I could love

there's also a bag of 100 pills in his flowered shirt pocket

it's fear and loathing in Costa Rica

and I'm cashing out.

CELEBRITIES

Leaving the cabin
in three weeks
what if the words stop?
I came here and drowned
couldn't get the words out fast enough
they flew by
keeping me from sleep
to scribble down a line
a title
for something there are no words for yet
but they will come

I'm a slave driver for the words
they live in the walls
knock abruptly
I'm lucky
10 months
sitting at this table
words
words
words
I've created like a mad woman
some of my best

I could give a damn how it's received
it's not why one should write

300 views, 600 thousand views

it doesn't matter

the only thing that matters is getting the words out so I can breathe

It pays better when the people like it

I like to eat—I guess

that's all it's worth

A friend told me the other day I had become a "figure"

a celebrity with a pen of sorts

why?

because someone you know

that I don't know

came across my words

on a dinky screen?

Celebrities are just people

I don't give a damn if someone is famous

I'll give the man the time of day bagging my groceries

or a rock star

all the same

we're all just doing our dance

The stars in your eyes are dangerous

yes, those—shed them

imaginary pedestals are useless

come down from there, darling

we're all down here

it's better here

A young woman replied to my cabin sublet ad

said she was "starstruck"

I was puzzled

flattered for a nanosecond

annoyed for a minute

then told her

I wake up like everyone else with Alice Cooper mosh pit hair

drool stains on my pillows

breath that smells like Khaosan Road

There are no celebrities

just people

doing the shit they love

or hate

sometimes people love what they love back

Then there's the people who value sitting next to said "celebrities"

who flake off

with a desperation that reeks

to be seen by cameras with no soul

be a corner in a beauty rag

We should wipe our asses with those
selling crap to those who will eat it
seek company that makes you rich
fills you
those ones
are the real celebrities.

There's assholes dancing

and there's assholes wishing they were dancing.

AND THIS IS HOW IT IS

we go home

and we shut our doors

we don't sleep with them open

for fear the world sees in

really sees us

sees our pain

sees our mess

sees the things we can't brush into place

the art we create we're too afraid to show the world

see our broken hearts

we don't open our doors wide

turn the spotlight on

and say, "I haven't done laundry in a week. My girlfriend
left me. I'm not sleeping."

we just shut the white door

with a blue handle

and lie in bed

staring at the ceiling all night.

I KEEP MY GRIEF IN A BOX

it's covered in duct tape

it's glued shut

I've tied it up with string

I've covered it in cement

I've hid it beneath the bed

so far below

that even I can't find it some days

Every once in a while

the box shows up

it opens itself

and takes me to the floor

sliding down a white fridge

and I try and tell it to go away

that I've already stopped

that I'm doing the best to live

that I don't have time for it tonight

that I can't do it right now

It opens itself up anyways

and takes me to my knees

and I want to cry and thrash and scream

but it's 9 o'clock on a Saturday and I'm living in suburbia

and if I scream and throw the dishes like I am in my head

someone will hear me and come

So I put on your songs

and I lie in sorrow and cry and cry and cry

until there is snot on my face

and my eyes are swollen and bright blue

and I just lie there

nothing will bring you back

and then I do my best to force my grief back into the box

hide all the things I can run into that remind me of you

and try to go on living for a little while longer.

I wish the world to smell like cedar. For the only struggle to be with spider webs from paths untouched by human feet. To fall asleep by a fire that cackles right there, on the floor, in the wood chips and the ash.

I wish to wake up each morning and pee in the woods. Brush my teeth looking out at a lake still sleeping. Spider webs glistening by a white bar of soap on the dock.

I wish to make kicking horse coffee in a blue tin cup and read book after book lying in the bottom of the canoe as it is still tied up.

I wish to wake up to the chill of the morning, not forced heat that makes me claustrophobic to breathe—crisp air, cleaned by the hemlocks and spruces outside my bedroom window.

I wish to wake up and water the flowers, barefoot and bare bummed. Light the kettle on a blue oven and pull open a door that stinks of cedar and time.

I would like you to be here, but if you're not—I will marvel, rest and play with the woman of the hour I came to see— mamma earth.

I am like a fish

in love with a bird

wishing I could fly

DID HE MAKE YOU COFFEE IN THE MORNING?

they come home
rumpled and frayed
hair full of fingers from the night before
back of the neck and hair dried with sweat
hours of sex all over their souls
we look up
and all know

I cock an eyebrow
"Did he make you coffee in the morning?"

The good ones own a silver espresso maker
they don't cheap out
buy the ground beans
you can tell in the color
too
if it's watery
a big brand name jug of cheap shit
or whole beans
reeking bitterly

The really good ones don't need to ask
they just open one eye
kiss the nape of your neck and say
"I'll make the coffee"

They know you take two creams

honey

and they walk you home after the coffee

proud to hold your hand and let the world know they loved you all night.

DOMESTICALLY DATING

You've heard the story

you go for a beer

next thing you know

she's got three brown suitcases

her pink square shampoo bottles in your shower

skip first dates

let's share toothbrushes

go grocery shopping

run errands

iron each other's clothes

get food poisoning and take care of one another

can you pass the toilet paper?

where's the iron?

laundry detergent?

meet the friends before we've stayed up all night having raunchy sex

you're a little chaotic

he says

you have no idea

scrubbing cold egg off the morning frying pan

CBC radio plays

Beethoven, Mozart, Bach

we could be wearing our matching slippers

stirring sugar and milk into white coffee cups

without making eye contact

because we've seen each other for the last 192 hours.

TOMORROW FEELS A LONG WAYS AWAY

Go away outside world

I do not understand you

Go away birds

Go away sunshine

Go away belly

I do not desire to eat

Go away work

Go away to-dos

Go away messages and phone calls

I cannot sleep any longer, and I do not wish to be awake

I do not wish to sit numbly beside the window and hear the garbage truck in the alley

I do not wish to hear the bee trapped in the window buzzing

and I do not wish to save him

sitting numbly all night listening to your songs

you are dead, yet you sing still for me

reading emails

reading messages

wondering why the fuck this is happening

what do we do now?

work?

I cannot work

there are no words I can write that are not heavy and sunken with the grief in my soul

I cannot write anything that will not reek heartache and loss

I cannot get in my car and go to the bank

I cannot move and walk and speak

I am stuck on a dead head floating in the water

I am stuck on music you wrote when you wished to die

I am stuck that you didn't hit the fucking emergency button

this is the lowest I have felt in my life

today, tomorrow feels a long ways away

where do I get the strength to go on?

where do I gather forgiveness?

where is my joy?

all I can see is pink and blue ribbons and a black walkie-talkie marked with a D.

THOSE EYES COULD MAKE A SANE WOMAN WILD & A WILD WOMAN SANE

I wish to remove the steel guitar from your fingers that strum

in the pale evening sun

I wish to place it on the floor

beside your brown boots

that have walked seven years

I want to know you

like those weathered boots do

I want to reach across the couch

and pull your head softly towards mine

I wish not to rush this

you are to be enjoyed

to be opened slowly

deliberately

carefully

I intend to kiss you

and before I do

I will write in circles about your eyes

for the ocean knows not of eyes that will make its beauty
shrink

and the stars have not seen their maker

the moon knows not of its match

but I do

those eyes

could make a sane woman wild

and a wild woman sane

I would like to lie for two hours in white sheets

'til they are crumpled and torn from three sides of the bed
with those green and hazel eyes.

I'M ON THE WAY TO KISS A MAN GOODBYE

He asks to come with me

he has a ride

I smile

like flies to honey

except the kind of flies you don't mind

tall

handsome

long-haired

non-Italian

six-foot-something flies

I'm on the way to kiss a man goodbye

and it's too soon to kiss another man hello

little fly

I see it in his eyes

then the words come

as I know they will

can I take you on a micro date?

ah

a micro date

where we look at the stars

fumble between kisses?

covered in sand on the beach?

swim in the ocean?

drink rum from the bottle?

collapse upon one another

wake to warm limbs and a sunrise?

I've done that little fly

and like I said

I've got a man to kiss goodbye

Can I just kiss you?

I laugh

I almost let him

drown in my honey

get drunk and dizzy

I hug him goodbye

tell him he can take me on a macro date if I ever make it
to New York.

I WILL NEVER BE A WELL-BEHAVED WOMAN

I would rather pass my days lying in the middle of dirt roads, staring at the full moon with a bottle of summer red in my palms.

I would rather have kids when it suits me, not when society expects or throws shoulds.

I would rather live in a hammock on a beach for six months, and write like my soul means it.

I would rather be horribly broke at times, than married to a job because a mortgage payment has my ass on a hook.

I would rather own moments, than investments.

I would rather eat alone, than sit with women who bore me at "Wives' Night."

I would rather swim naked with bioluminescence, have it fall like fireflies from my hair, my breasts, my back.

I would rather do handstands naked in the moonlight when no one's watching than pick bridesmaid dresses.

I would rather drink seven-year-old rum from a sandy bottle, smell of smoke and ash than sit in church.

I would rather learn from life than rack up debt, in a desk.

I would rather drink the ocean, again and again—celebrate being madly alive.

I would rather my love be defined by love itself, and nothing more or less.

I do not need a ring on my finger to prove that I am in love.

I would rather take the chicken bus, than spend useless money in safe-gated communities.

Sit beside a goat, listen to reggaeton and eat green mango with sugar in a plastic bag sold from the woman who harasses the bus each time it stops.

I do not need a degree to prove that I am intelligent.

I do not need to own a piece of earth with some wood on top of it—to feel successful. No one truly owns the land, anyway—we just think we do.

My savings account has diddly to do with my richness.

I would rather sprawl my single ass out like a lioness each morning and enjoy each corner of my empty bed.

I will take a job I love and freedom over a pension, any day.

I will not work and work and work to live when my body is old and I am tired.

Stocks are for people who get boners from money.

Not everyone should have kids, and my eggs aren't expiring.

I will not drink the societal Kool-Aid on a bus, nor will I drink it on a train.

Not on a plane, with a goat, in the rain, in the dark, in a tree, with a fox, in a box!

I will not jump through society's hoops and red tape, the treasure hunt in the rat race we chase.

If we must have milestones—mine will be measured by how much joy I have collected at the end of each day and how often in this life I have truly, deeply, opened.

Seek, see, love, do.

I WISH TO REST INTO YOU

my love

possibly collapse

and I know we mustn't

fall

for we must hold ourselves

before we hold

each other's

warm bodies

in the night that bites

where lovers lay

but tonight

my love

I would like to collapse

I would like to exhale

and with it

let go

of all my fire

all the do's

I would like to be a child

in your arms

and be held

as if I could break.

TO MY LOVER I HAVEN'T QUITE MET YET

I'd like for you to visit

I say softly

will you come in August?

August is the fall of summer

each ray of sunshine is fleeting and bittersweet

on its way out

demanding of you to love it even more so because of it

Night nudges gently of fall's arrival

wool sweaters and socks come out of the closets

I cut kindling for the fire

my hands rediscovering the axe, knots and the smell of
freshly cut cedar

The euphoria has worn away by then

we don't run to each other with eyes made of love and stars

instead we lie beside each other on the dock at dusk

you bring a bottle of bourbon

and I'll build a boat

we can pretend to fish

with no real desire to catch or not catch anything

and I'll read us poetry

as we gaze at the sky

for our love isn't hurried

it doesn't shy away unsure

we've played, made love, had second doubts and made

love again
I choose you and you choose me
and we meet here, together

I curl into your t-shirt
the soft one
and press my ice-cold feet against your legs
you yelp with shock
and pull away before pulling me closer
into your red beating heart
to warm the night away

We leave the lights on
and read for a little while
the moon is so distracting I don't get much done
but you do
you wear glasses
shirtless, letting your hairy bear chest free
yellow beeswax candles burn softly
I hold you in my eyes
for my heart is paying attention.

TO MY LOVER I HAVEN'T QUITE MET YET (PART II)

I'd like to lie with you

and for each time we undress to marvel at the newness of
each other's skin

to be the lovers that drink up love

like they're starving

tasting stars and drinking moonlight

I'd like to kiss you when the moon is full, or new or a quarter

it doesn't really matter

I just want those lips

I'd like for it to rain

and listen to the tink tink

as I count stars

or for it to not rain and be sunny

I'd like to hold you

not because I'm cold

but because I want to lie beside you

I'd like to love you when the sun comes up

to bathe in our light

to drink coffee tangled in a messy joyous heap

I'd like to make raspberries on your back and tickle you 'til
you shove me off the bed

I'd like to start the day laughing

And I'd like to make love to you

right there

on the floor

for my intent is to drink your existence.

I'LL TAKE MY COFFEE WITH A SIDE OF YOU

My hair falls softly
caressing the curves of my shoulder
the smell of coffee runs up the stairs to greet you
hummingbirds hover
saying soft hellos to the flowers woven upon my balcony

I push the French press down
slowly
letting the grains resist my urgency
just milk, he says
pitter patter falls the rain
Jose Gonzalez fills the kitchen
my denim shirt falls open
carelessly buttoned
I shiver
the sun has not yet reached my cabin
and the logs still hold the night

The rain falls gently, then fast
like Mother Nature's fingertips
drumming away on the roof
where did the inside sheet run off to?
I pull you close
we are too tangled to start a fire
drinking each other's body heat
murmuring nonsensical romance

Nine days?

it can't be

the creek beside my cabin rushes wildly

tormented by the rain

a woodpecker drills away in the distance

all I feel is your lips drift upon my purple nipples

my soul curls

gasps in sweet delight

tightens itself

and lets go into the abyss

strength within surrender

kissing away hours

fingertips glide between thighs

pillows astray

as we meet between the sheets

I find your mouth

again and again and again

He leaves fresh cut wildflowers on every windowsill

purple lilies on the doorstep

whittles the day away

palms full of splinters

my heart warms quietly in my chest

can one eat kisses?

I'm starving for your lips

and they just left mine.

COME TO MEXICO WITH ME

the words exit his mouth

and enter my heart

all in one breath

six days

and we are already three months ahead

can I keep you?

I ask

swigging the last bottle of tequila in this town

fetched on a green bicycle

by a man

that all my heart is running

face first

into loving.

I AM SAD THIS MORNING
the yellow sunflowers are sad

my cold toes upon the hardwood floor are sad

the roses refuse to smell sweetly this morning

and my blue heart aches

for I am unable to open

I am unable to crack my heart in my chest for you

and how I wish to

if one could boss me into love

it would be you

if there was one person I wish I could open to

it would be you

and I'm not sure if I am for you

and you deserve to be loved richly

wholly

not in small flutters

so this morning my heart aches slowly and sadly in my chest.

AN ITALIAN ONCE TOLD ME
there is very little
between good poetry
and bad poetry
he says
blowing smoke
mixed with marijuana
into the night
filled with crickets and loneliness

Each time the pen falls
I wonder if the poem will be
good
or
shit
suppose I'll never know
so I'll just keep writing.

SOMETIMES HITCHHIKING IS OKAY
AND SOMETIMES IT ISN'T

Sometimes you wind up

in the back of a pick-up truck

with two black dogs

one kid

a few rice sacks

The back of a moto

eating dust

happy

in the sunshine

the worst they do

is ask if you have a boyfriend

you lie

smile

say goodbye

Sometimes the man who picks you up

in a silver SUV

with blond hair

sunglasses to mask eyes

that would've stopped you asking for the ride

and you stay calm

knowing next time

to listen closely to your gut

I write stories

he says

fiction?

I ask

nonfiction?

real life

he replies

my life is crazy

no need to make anything up

I don't need to ask

but I do

we have a distance to cross

and I've heard the best way to make friends with someone

is to let them talk about themselves

Short stories

about a guy who robbed me

so I locked him up

messed him up real bad

the cops came

his family came

no one fucks with me anymore

I'm armed

It's not safe for you

for women here

So, it's a true story?

yes, I told you so

he lets me out

safe

sometimes hitchhiking is okay and sometimes it isn't.

IT'S JUST SEX

he says
my heart's in a box
and it won't come out
it did for a little while with you
I felt
but it's back in there
and it's not coming out

It would be quite complicated to meet me
if you weren't a feeler
I'm all the feels
all the time

I still try to love those ones sometimes
the ones who aren't ready to be loved
who crack their hearts open a little
let me in for a week
maybe two
and then run into the night
for empty legs
and solitude in a bed
that is vacant of love
where their hearts won't be bothered

I still lie awake and think of you
which is sad really

you're likely in a pillow

full of blonde hair

that smells like sex

and I spend the night trying to compose a key

with my words

to unlock your heart for good.

APPARENTLY I WRITE THE BEST POEMS

when I'm hungover

after 4 hours' sleep

two glasses of wine

tequila

Chivas

neat

fucking a man

with blond hair

in a ponytail

with blue eyes

on white concrete

before I never see him again.

EVERY TIME THE PLANE SHAKES

enough that the fasten seat belt sign

blinks on

and "Please return to your seats"

plays overhead

I point my finger at the Gods

and say strictly

I have a lot of bad ass shit to create still

I am not

going down

like

this

you hear?

and then the plane settles

and I take a sip of my shitty airplane coffee

with a red plastic straw to the left

this life is for living

I am a visionary juicing our world to create the sustenance
of my dreams

there is no time to go down
until I have lit this world on fire with my art.

ENLIGHTENED TOILET PAPER

I don't want to write love ballads
enlightened toilet paper
full of insights and ahas
there are frogs wearing crowns
they have built with their egos
croaking to people who are drinking the spiritual Kool-Aid
of the 21st century

I am bored over here
reading wannabe Rumi's
so what shall I write now?
love is grande
romanticism is a fairytale I can build easily in my head
but what of truth?

I would rather tell you
quit the degree
fuck the piece of paper
if you're not going to use it get up and leave
you don't need it

You don't need the house
you don't need the diamond
you might die before you reap the benefits of that pension
you don't need the child
unless you want to stay up listening to screaming 'til 4 AM

to give your mother a granddaughter

dogs are better kids anyway

skip the minivan

fuck suburbia

screw Costco

pick up what gives you joy

and put down everything else

I would rather piss off the blue collars

twist the panties of the white collars

confuse the beliefs of those who have chameleoned their
beliefs from their parents

why do you believe that?

you were only meant to adopt the genetics of your parents

not their closed-mindedness

not their fear

Don't simply continue doing something

just because you're successful at it

you can be good at all kinds of things

be good at what gives you joy

Question it all

you have a law degree

good for you

if it makes you unhappy

leave

You've bought a house with a big ol' white fence

that wraps around the block

stinking of money

lean back against it

one day with a push lawnmower

and realize you don't want this life

sell it

give it away

we are only prisoners if we fall victim to the choices we have
made that are parched dry of the authenticity of our souls

I will go out

burning like a light on my deathbed

shouting bullshit

at the falsity of this world

and I will continue to do so

every day until then

with my pen.

I am fire

if you want something salty and sweet

with no opinion

I am not the woman for you

I spit flames

often.

I am the tenderloin
of New York steaks
and you fell
and slipped your dick
in a striploin.

More men like you than any woman I know
yes
but none of them want to keep me.

POEMS ARE WHERE THE PAIN GOES

I do not write poetry with a heart full of joy
I write the sorrow so that it can be kept somewhere
other than my heart
I write of my pain when I am left
I write of my anger at the wrongs I see on this planet
I write of love that does not become love
but instead is flushed down the toilet
left unread

I write loneliness
I write blind with rage
I write the justice I do not see
I write the ribs of the orange dog
begging for chicken who is not fed a bone
and falls asleep hungry

The poetry that falls from these hands
is not a love story with doors being opened
first kisses that smell like expensive perfume

These poems are large bites of purple lips
that are found in the limbs of sex
that is useless and empty of love

These poems rise from the trenches of despair
heartache, confusion, grief
and pretend to be fierce and strong

meanwhile I shiver and quake
stay awake at night
peacocking a liberation
drowned in falsity
hopeful strength only in validation

I am not strong
I am hurt
licking my wounds
alone
always alone
with my pen

Do not be fooled
poets are cowards
who turn weakness into a dance
heartache into independence
loneliness into courage

It's all yellow tail feathers
lies and deceit
we are all heartbroken and loveless
grasping for control over that which we can never control
with our pens
and you are the puppets we pull at the bottom of the strings
how does it feel down there?

you may taste bites of my world

but I am up here weaving a story

you will never truly see

Oh yes

you are digesting regurgitated experiences down there

so you never know

even when you think you know

you are simply knowing an experience of an experience

Am I strong?

or am I alone?

is my sadness beautiful or it is a pain so deep you would leave if you could see?

am I empowered or am I afraid?

Today I will let you in

I am afraid of intimacy

I choose the ones who are empty of love

to validate the victimization of my fatherless pain

I truly wish a knight

I truly wish to be kept close to a heart that beats

yet I fight the ones who try and love me

and chase the ones who never will

and then I write pretty little poems

which are full of pain to you

and it continues.

Forgive me hands
for I have held
everything
but my self.

HE IS HERE

I want to wake up beside you

the words exit my brain

onto blue and white cotton sheets

full of elephants

and quiet my heart

I feel as if I've eavesdropped on something I shouldn't know just yet

but they are here

they are here in an all-white café

with a man who feels like a magnet

all the dust

motorcycles yelling

fall away

they are here on a green bicycle

through glacier eyes

in a photograph

they are here in a way that makes me wonder if any of the men I've kissed

or loved

or kept

have really made sense

for every molecule in my being smiles when I think of him

and I don't wish to know

to understand

I just know he's here

and that I look forward to rolling over

on a Tuesday afternoon

and seeing closed eyelashes

his blond hair

and hearing a red heart that beats beside me

in these blue and white sheets.

So, what's your job?

I take slabs of my heart and share them with the world for a living.

I'm not sure if I'm more afraid

of being loved

or being left

sounds like you've had a lot of left stories

and not a lot of love stories.

They did not take your power
you gave it to them
don't give it to them.

What they don't tell you as a little girl

in the fairytale books

is that sometimes you kiss a frog

and it turns into a prince

and you spend three hot years with him in love

and then one day

he cheats on you

and turns back into a toad

and you must chuck him back in the pond

and just keep fucking swimming.

You can't even make eye contact with me
no
he says
I'm terrified to look at you
because I could fall in love with you
in 24 hours

So instead he sticks his dick
in empty holes
void of meaningful connections
and numbs with cigarettes, cocaine and whisky.

It is as if there is a heat

pulling me

from the waist

into him

we are talking and moving and my hands move an orange
fork towards my mouth

yet a part of my soul has climbed into him

I am on top of him

with the wetness in between my thighs

with my tongue against his tongue

like vines

discovering the heat of our mouths

his hands underneath my layers

fumbling and falling with excitement at the softness of a
skin unfelt

I can barley take it

yet I nod and take another bite of chicken vindaloo and
stare out at the white of the ocean

and pretend there is not a magnet of energy between our
bodies

requesting me to throw the agreements I have and haven't
made into the wind or the ocean and dive in.

WHAT KIND OF WOMAN ARE YOU?

he asks over a shirt that is blue with red Hawaiian flowers

his open hairy chest breathing

into the conversations that hum

beside a yellow half moon

in a rocky restaurant

full of green plastic chairs

I smile

blow the grey smoke of a cigar

through my stained red lips

I believe in dessert before dinner

I pray that Christians break up with Christ

throw their purity rings off a bridge

marriage disgusts me

politics bore me

children irritate me

I wipe my ass with newspapers

shit full of fear

I think religion is all the same

we just change the name of the one we worship

If I had a father and he died I would spend his will on hookers and cocaine

I drink more coffee than water

I like when men lick me in circles

tease me between my second lips

I'll kiss the inside of your thighs
that have never seen sunlight
licking and moving slowly up your waist
taking all of you in my mouth
before the sun is awake

I shimmy and shake my hips low
for I love to feel the power of the earth
between my legs

I scare the shit out of those who are lying to themselves
and attract those who wouldn't dare
but hesitate
drowned in shameful curiosity
I keep company only of those
that
are

If you leave me
I pause
take a sip of a silver can
full of some beer barely worth drinking
flashing my blue eyes in the dark
I'll be fine
he smiles
waves
we'll get the cheque.

He rips my white body suit to the side
in a parking lot
under the night sunshine of traffic lights
and sticks two fingers inside of me
it isn't the hole that needs filling
but it'll do.

I would like to lie

hip locked with you

until the dusk crickets

and the drunk roosters roar.

I AM A WOMAN OF DISTINCTION

Recklessly beautiful and untamed—my heart is splayed wide open for I not only trust the process, but I trust the force in which each one of my feet hits the ground and my ability to maneuver through the joys and grief I face each day.

I walk tall, taller than an old cypress tree because I am at home in my skin—my self-worth lives in each nook and cranny of my spine.

It is not attached to exterior what-have-you's like money, a piece of paper, a house, a car, this world's approval, a ring or success.

My success is in presence.

I am present in the humans I stumble upon like heartbeats at first light and in the night.

I salsa dance bare bummed with bronze skin and white cheeks—let the music sway and bend and dip my spirit with the grace of a dozen fireflies drunk on the moon's wine.

I am dripping in salt, browned from the sunshine and barefoot in my beauty.

I am not afraid to tell you that I am beautiful because I have done the work to be at home in my soul's skin.

I do not shrink to accommodate the insecurities of those around me, but stand tall to remind them gently, why crouch?

My body may be a meat bag, a vessel for the magnificence I hold inside but I cherish each scar on my chin, each freckle, each voluptuous sun bleached curl, each inch of my breasts.

I walk with my head held high when I walk into a room because I know there is space for me in this world—however I may come.

I show this world my tears and my laughter, unashamed.

I know better than to try and fix or heal the suffering of this world.

I know that by healing my suffering, I heal this world.

I am a woman of distinction and I am not afraid to love you before you are ready.

I am not afraid to move faster or slower than the expectations we lay on vulnerability and opening.

I open at my will.

I open at the first drop of a breeze, at a smile from the man sitting with a green top hat that I pass in a taxicab.

I open fearlessly and sweetly and ferociously with all the might I can for what good is living if we are not loving?

I am here to love and love I will.

I am a woman of distinction, and I am not a victim of circumstance—I feel when things are out of alignment and I move from them with as much grace as I enter.

I show up for this world.

I set boundaries with ease that honor me.

I understand that no is self-love and everything after no is unworthiness.

I am worthy, darling—oh so deliciously worthy.

I am authentic as all hell and can taste bullshit from a mile away.

I spit out societal Kool-Aid laughing and write my own bible.

I ground—ground through movement, through dance, through the sea.

I drink the ocean for breakfast and kiss the red dirt for dessert.

I do not keep my freedom in a cage that requires six whiskies to be let loose.

I dance and shimmy and shake and love through my life.

I am a woman of distinction—you will feel me when I walk into the room.

I could have stayed
that morning
and kissed you
until August.

IF I GET LONELY, I'LL POUR AN ARDBEG UIGEADAIL AND MASTURBATE

And some of the men

show up

charming

with grandiose gestures

with big promises of vaulting moments

and then slink off

into the night

like the black cat

I read about in that children's book

never to be seen again

and I just sit

on a white staircase

hitting the butt of a cigarette

into a tin can

watching the roundness of the moon

that is not quite full

and go

fuck

where did that one go?

and I know

I drive them into the night

running screaming in the daylight

as if there is coal under their feet

because I breathe a fire

that not many men can stomach

and all these new agey

bullshit courses

say I'm too masculine

and that I need to embrace my feminine

furnish my house with a pink blanket

walk in my hips

receive

not pursue

but I am what I am

and in the daytime I am building a fucking empire

that requires a facilitator

and a doer

and a mover

a shaker who makes choices

with her gut

I am not a minion

that sits quietly on the sidelines

I am up at night under the covers

creating plans of attack

of how to throw my art ferociously and impactfully into this world

so no

I am not in the kitchen

using a pink bowl

stirring cupcake batter

and being in my feminine

and sometimes I facilitate the fuck out of love

and try and make the moves

because I don't have time to sit around and be pursued

I'm taking bites of this world

with each exhale

out of my stained red lips

so I guess

if they run

into the night

I can smack their ass

on the way out

and find a man who likes to be chosen

who likes to be pursued right back

and if he doesn't

well, fuck him

I'll just sit here and smoke cigarettes

in between building a goddamn empire

and taking over this world

and if I get lonely

I'll pour an Ardbeg Uigeadail

and masturbate.

DEAR MEN

if a woman smiles at you

slyly

like she knows some secret you have only brushed up against

in the dreams that are sometimes sweet

yet always fleeting

run

run as far away as you can

for she just wants to

eat your heart

from the inside out

and finish your soul off for dessert.

HIS JOB

He sacrificed himself for you

in this life

so you could learn how you deserve to be loved

his job

was to love the soles of your feet that have never felt the ground

his job

was to love your lungs that had been drinking water

not knowing they needed air

his job

was to give your body the rest and the release of pleasure it had given up on

his job

was to allow you to feel the rise and fall and shudder as you experienced the joy within making love

yes

making love

love

love

not sex

his job

was to awaken the parts of your spirit that were not aware they were sleeping

his job was to pull you out from under the bed

so you could see your whole light

his job

was to remind you that loving you is not a burden

but everything he was born on this planet to do

for his hands were forged to hold you

each inch of your flesh and red beating heart

with soft might

his job was not to be with you forever

no

his job was to be the one who loved you so sweetly and so
deeply that you are unable to deny the love you denied yourself

your whole life.

They drink me
like water they do not know they need
and buzz to me like flies drunk off honey
because I am a real thing
in this fake world.

Quit distracting me

wait

do

do distract me

because I've waited for twenty-six years

for the stars to shimmy

the moon to make her moves

the sun to redden

after the fourth eclipse

for you to walk into my life

and steal every ounce of attention

I ever had and ever will.

WHY ISN'T HE HERE?

I ask the rum

or the couch

or the heater that creaks as it slows down at 10:28 PM

on a Saturday night

because you're not ready

I reply

oh, alright

and I walk across the old hardwood floor

and floss my teeth of leftover basil

from pasta

and go to sleep

without sex

I miss the sex

it's been 3 months

there's cobwebs on my vagina

but sex without love

is like banging your funny bone

it just doesn't hit the spot.

You know what going mad takes?

a bottle of rosé wine

a Tuesday night

and a man who says he doesn't miss your presence.

THE POET IN ME

can see you writing me

saying

I was afraid

I ran away

I'm sorry

I told you I usually run away, do you remember?

and I would

and I would forgive you with urgency

for it's the most right

right has ever felt

so far

and I have run from love

more times than I would like to admit

I can see myself landing in Puerto Vallarta

in two weeks

with brown and blonde curls as big as the Indian Ocean

toppling over one another with excitement to see you

I can feel the trickle of sweat

under a white shirt that is unbuttoned three times

billowing in the breeze

that comes when you're a poet and can paint it all at your palms

I can see you

and your glacier blues

waiting for me

there

you're wearing that light blue shirt
and you are different but the same
hearts don't age like cheese or nice wine
but we do

I can see myself laughing with your parents
your dad brushing the grey of his hair
your mother likes me
all mothers like me
I have a kind heart
you do too

I see us on airplanes
packing toothbrushes and laptops
telephone calls late at night when we are gone
we may go places
but it doesn't
it
won't
for when it is real
it vibrates and hums quietly in the night
through the days
over oceans and mountains and cities blowing black fog
into the trees

Yes, I'm going there

I can see us on a small yellow float plane flying over the green and blues

there's a yellow large mop of a dog with a rusted collar

a blue 6'4" retro fish

perhaps a fishing rod

I've never been fishing you know

My fingers loosely hold yours

I can see us sleeping in a green tent

in Fryatt Valley

cold toes pressed against your legs

I would like to take you there

I would like to show you Canada someday

not right now

you're not ready

but someday I would like to show you all kinds of things

drink coffee in a blue tin can and shower in the yellow and pink limestone waterfall

we will need to hoist our food up every night into a tree

for bears and cougars

you'd like that

I can see you chopping wood

through a window that has seen twenty years of rain

I can see a wool grey blanket and a roaring fire

fed by cedar

I can see my heart burning beside it

for you light a fire in me

I can see the back of your blond head on a white pillow
underneath a bug net beside me

I can feel the weight of your arm as you wake up and pull
me inside you

I can even see you sitting next to me

on this blue seat

today

in 32 F

passing by the turquoise greens of Miami

watching white clouds and a world pass by

we would drink black coffee

and I would massage your right hand

that you hurt

as you are as hard on your body

as this is on my heart

The poet in me can see all of these things

for I have the imagination of Picasso and the fingers of Frida

I can go anywhere with my heart and these words

it is why I breathe

but you are right

there is only black coffee

and I am alone

missing you foolishly and sweetly

writing this poem.

I AM COLLECTING MEN
like flower petals
in Bali
pink ones
white ones
they lay in my bed
stomach breathing into the night
hair stinking of salt
bodies full of a warmth
I wish to drink and drink
like an endless cup
I am collecting white teeth
smiles
hair flying by
on a scooter as the world passes by.

I am surprised to see so many beautiful girls traveling alone
he says
brave doesn't have a gender
I say.

FORGET COLLEGE

find mentors

to work with

beside

under

for

who teach you their ways

wisdom is experience

books only give you knowledge

the importance of the piece of paper is retiring

university is like the military

we don't need it

I promise

we're just spoonfed bullshit

of fear

of validation

qualify yourself to follow your dreams

write your own piece of paper with each stroke of your life

you don't need a desk

or a $30,000 loan

instead find those who catch your spirit and learn from
them as much as you possibly can.

I AM MY OWN CUP OF TEA

I am easy to love

like water to your body

air to your lungs

sunshine to your skin

I am composed of a soul sweat you have surely never tasted

of stories and skin that Zeus reached down from the heavens and sewed himself

of sweetness and thighs and lips that men have painted

and will continue to talk about and make art about when I am grey and this world is young

I encompass paint brushes that live in my brain that speak daily the wonders and sorrows of this world

I do not discuss people or events, I discuss intentions that I walk with fire and bravery and might

there is curiosity and relentless joy in the left corner of my eye

and a wide-open heart in a love story with this world in my right

it doesn't matter if you drink me

I am my own cup of tea.

AFTER YOU

What are you doing to me?

I am like a teenager

he grabs the flesh of my ass with his entire mouth

I laugh loudly

why is this funny?

I'm serious

what will there be after you?

you have the most feminine body I have ever touched

I'm going to need to become a nun

after you

because nothing can compare to this.

Who says feminists hate men?

I love men

the only bashing of men I do is with my vagina.

TRUSTAFARIAN

he asks

no

welfare

I reply

but maybe if I had a trust fund

I could have built my castle faster

so I could invite all the trolls up for tea

Would you like a cup?

or would you like to stay down there

and continue to yell your projections

insecurities

and fear

on my walls?

He drops his head

sugar

please

I hand him a brown cup of tea

My mom...

I know

I reply

we are all wounded children yelling at this world for the love we did not receive from our parents

he lifts the right side of his face in silent agreement

and we stir our tea.

You have little feet

he says

you know what they say about little feet

I reply

what?

he asks confused

little vaginas.

I FEEL HIS HAND UPON MY LEG

I felt his eyes

before his hand

I feel his words

before he speaks them

his black hood is covering half his face

his abs breathe in the night

what do you write?

poetry

about what?

would you like to read one?

I ask

will you read it to me?

no, that's why I'm a writer

he laughs

I hand him

'mamma didn't raise no fucking princess'

he reads it

he hands it to the woman with white hair and glass frames
next to him

you're liberal

he says

you have no idea

the lifeguard who saw me surf naked at 10 AM today

has an idea.

I believe that a woman is born with a type of orgasm
and a type of a kiss
his words echo on a white rooftop in Fuerteventura
I hold those words in beautiful stillness in my heart
for truth rings like church bells
no matter the day
the moment
drinking clarity is something we cannot deny ourselves
when it comes.

I MUST GIVE IT TO THEM SLOWER

shouldn't I?

it is a question that desires more than silence

I open the iron locks on my wooden window and speak to
the yellow moon

your heart?

she replies

as she smokes a drag of a passing shooting star

oh dear

no

give it as slowly or as fast as it happens

we are all making marks on souls

with the teeth of our hearts

and if they cannot handle a bite they do not deserve a kiss.

BE YOUR OWN GODDAMN KNIGHT

Love isn't coming to sweep you off your feet—it isn't.

Don't sit by the door and listen for the hum of a black motorcycle as it makes its way to your doorstep—he's not coming.

He's not coming on a horse or a plane, by bike or on his feet—he's not coming.

He's not coming to say the things you want to hear in the crevices of your open heart—he's not ready yet.

He's not coming to bury you in the whites of your pillows and rest his head in the softness of your breasts—he's too busy chasing a dream that does not carry the flesh and heat and heart of love.

He is not ready for a woman of heart who cries with each beat that she opens.

He's not coming to put a ring on your finger and a baby in your belly—he's too busy chasing sex and drugs and women who are passing to need to feel the tangibility of tenderness.

He's not coming to bring you another half of you—so be the whole fucking thing.

Don't sit on the sidelines and think that love will be the band aid of the loneliness that sneaks in—be alone.

Be wildly, deliciously alone.

Sweep your own ass off its feet.

I DID NOT BRING YOU HERE TO MAKE LOVE TONIGHT

I do not wish you to remove the blackness of my bra and taste my pink flesh with your lips.

I did not call upon you to press my breast upon your breast and tongue-kiss into the night.

I did not ask you to meet me, so we could re-dance a dance we've done. I know where you step and I stand.

The love we made was sweet and salty and there are poems and songs and art that we will have tangibly, long after I have left this cabin and you are gone.

They are written and hang from the walls, the ceilings, the old hardwood floors that creak. They are in the moans, in the red candle wax with no wicks left.

They are in the records that we've played, the wine that we've drank and the bed that I sleep in.

They surface like black and white movies, reeling slowly in my brain when I hear your left shoe fall on the floor.

Although we have been lovers, and could be again, I did not bring you here to make love.

I brought you here to love me.

Not with your lips or your hands, your brown arms with hair golden from the spring sun, but your heart.

I brought you here to peer into your soul and see if we are a love story worth breathing on the embers for.

If I wish to open my heart, to you, again.

If we have more to write and say and do and be and go and live and love.

So, no, I do not wish you to carry me, leaving my white cotton shirt upon the banister to the bedroom we have made love in.

My skin smells of coconut and I know we would make love so sweetly the moon may reach for a cloud to cover her ears, for she cannot bear to know such a thing.

I do not wish you to kiss the skin above my waist with your tongue. I do not wish you to embrace me with those arms.

I do not wish you to think me naked. Sex is easy and love is hard.

So do not reach for me with lust that is expiring as the dusk crickets move through yellow spring flowers in the fields below.

Do not bring your desires empty of a sweetness that lasts to my doorstep. I am waiting for love.

And although I am free, and a lover of passion and sex without shame or judgment—just for the heat in my belly and warmth in between my legs—I do not wish to have sex with you tonight.

I may not need a ring, or white dresses, or papers with signatures—but there is one thing I need from you tonight.

So come here, if you will, so I may hold you, beside my red beating heart and the crackling of the fire.

But you must promise to toss away the lust and the wishes and the wants.

I am waiting to hold someone in my heart, before I take them between my freckled thighs.

We aren't afraid of heights; we are afraid of falling. We aren't afraid of love, we're afraid of being heartbroken—of anguish, of being alone. We aren't afraid of intimacy—we're afraid if we show our whole selves to this world the world won't like it. That once we are open we may be left. We aren't afraid of flying—we're afraid of not having control if something goes wrong, we're afraid of dying.

Darling, I hope you risk. I hope you fall so you can only see the jump wasn't as big as you thought it was. I wish the ground to hit your feet and see your smile and your tears when you discover the space that was there all along.

Darling, I hope you love—love so hard you may grieve for years and not because you're weak or you're soft but because you opened your heart with ferocious might and once the salt of the tears has run from your blood I wish you to exhale and fall into the heart of someone new.

Risk—darling, risk.

I'M NOT BUILT FOR THE CITY

I'm ungrounded by the red cars, yellow taxicabs whizzing by, the people honking, their car windows unrolled and music blasting.

Cigarette smoke being blown from red painted lips in front of bars with beer-stained carpets that reek of the unloved.

I'm put off by the people rushing, no one stopping, no one looking up, no one smiling and saying hello, staring into screens—no connecting.

I spoke with a woman waiting for the streetcar who told me she is tired, that her job doesn't fill her, that she thinks that's just how it is—it's not how it is, I wanted to say. But I didn't.

I'm on a subway with blue velvet seats with teenage boys watching YouTube videos, frying their brains with bullshit.

I'm sitting next to a woman who has polished each hair on her head, each eyelash on her face—I wonder if she feels beautiful. I wonder if she is happy. I wonder if she knows she doesn't need to spend so much time perfecting, that she's beautiful before it all—right as she wakes, as-is. I hope someone in her life tells her she is beautiful every day.

I don't remember how to dress myself for the city. I don't want to wear shoes. I don't wish to walk fast. I don't wish to push to get on the subway train. I don't wish to smell McDonald's and see ties and polished shoes in line at chain coffee shops with overpriced coffee.

I don't wish to blend into a sea of people existing without stopping to see one another.

Perhaps I live alone in the woods because in cities such as these, we live close to be alone.

The people sitting on the beach throwing Frisbees, running, making sand castles, with dogs—they have no idea. There's politics, rip currents, large black and white spotted stingrays that leap in front of you—flying like god through the morning air.

Surfers have a world, an earth, a doorway that isn't understood unless you've been here—out past the chaos of the whitewash, out where the blue and green ripples hum across the ocean towards you in the pink and gold morning light like Zeus has taken his wand and beckoned the sky to fall and dance for you.

The ocean is my favorite coffee shop—it's where I meet my friends, my lovers—it's where I get a degree in philosophy on small days where I talk to the man beside me who's a cello player and has toured the world and slept beneath dusty staircases.

Out here is an existence between a forbidden world for humans, where we would otherwise collect water in our lungs—where I cheat, and play with dolphins and fish and they stare up dumbly because we aren't meant to know— or be here, and yet we are and I am and I understand.

What time is it in Sweden?

10:30 AM

he replies

so I am in the future

by one hour

you are my future

he replies.

The samba plays

and the golden hills roll

and he whistles

I love the ass of a woman so much

that if a woman has a beautiful ass

and I am taking her from behind

I must think so hard about her heart

and her beautiful spirit

or I loose myself

and let go

and I don't I want to let go

for sex is a spiritual experience

then he turns the knob to the right

and the music plays

and the wind blows hot into the car

through the mountains and green sea of Spain.

I am choosing women to be around

that need me

he remarks

yes

why are you choosing to spend your time in the company
of lambs

when you could be sitting amongst lions?

MY WORLD IS STANDING AND TALL

I am an old cypress tree
I do not shake by the opinions of others
I do not bend at their whispers
I do not stretch to hear their approval
nor hide from their judgment
their thoughts are theirs alone

My power is here
in my belly
roaring with all its might

Swing, swing, swing
raging through the night
and the sunlight
but you cannot take my power
it lies here
inside of me

I choose to walk smaller
I choose to walk taller
I choose when I kneel
when I fall

You may swing left
you may swing right
you cannot hit me
you see?
walk away and leave me be.

IF THERE IS LOVE HEAR THE LOVE

if there is an uproar

monkeys flinging their shit projections

so be it

do not rush to shake the hands of those who love

and do not get on your knees to clean the shit of others

let your head explode long enough to know why you're
doing it then whack it down

hard

back to earth

and remind yourself you know nothing

the earth is moving

even when we are standing still

there is no certainty

truths change

and are not always shared

write your truth

but do not shove your truth on others

listen to the praise only enough to shield from the blows

listen to the blows only to gain inspiration to write more

if the blows are too low

forget listening

it's not about you

be a membrane

let it all pass

to sleep deep

and wake up to write like a motherfucker in the morning.

I AM NOT A HUMBLE GRASSHOPPER

If you have forgotten who I am
and where I came from
let me remind you
I am not a humble grasshopper
I am a mountain lion
I do not bounce lightly when people are not accountable
I do not walk away
I turn my prey on their backs like a porcupine
slice open their exposed underbellies
I am patient
I am a powerful hunter
I will not go away
fade into the distance
so you may run
with your enlightened tail
quivering between your legs
into the woods
for as long as you so wish
but when you return
know I will be waiting.

I'M ON IT

Hey!

I whistle down the line

I'm on it

the men one by one pull their boards from the wave

Hey!

I'm here

I'm taking up space

for women have taken no space for centuries

and men

take and take and take

and women voiceless

married to a man named Pablo

who drinks from 7 AM until the night

and beats her first with his fists

and then with his dick

for it is not love fucking

it is just a dick getting hard ramming into a hole that doesn't have a voice

Hey!

I'm taking this wave

for the fourteen-year-old married away to a man twice her age

who cries in the field by her parents' house for she dreamed of a love that is loving

a love that is choice

Hey!

I'm taking this wave

for the countries who short women education

who short women the same goddamn pay just because they have lips in between their legs

Hey!

I'm taking this wave

for the women who when they were raped were asked

"What were you wearing?"

Hey!

I'm taking this wave

for myself

for the men in business suits who would come into the restaurant I worked at and leer drunkenly at me

while attempting to caress my leg

Hey!

I'm taking this wave for all of the times I was an object

and not the brilliant fucking brain I am

Hey!

I'm taking this wave for the time in Greece

a man dropped his pants when I walked by in a bikini and jacked off in broad daylight

watching my young body walk away

Hey!

I'm taking this wave

because the policemen I called didn't give a fuck and the women I went to crying laughed at me

Hey!

today

I am taking this wave

for a lifetime of women not being heard

not being listened to

not getting a space in the room

and today you must take the spray of my feet in your face.

DO NOT COME TO THE MOUNTAIN
AND REFUSE TO FEEL HER

The earth twerked

the yellow wasps stung

angry at the feet that fell loudly on the red earth of their
land

the tarantula withdrew

because secretly she knew

that we cannot fathom

the greatness

of her red hollow thighs

the white cum of commercialization

and soul prostitution

plastic consumption

car guzzling gasolined frenzied greed

get out

says the mountain

get out and take your photographs

and your lack of presence

absence of honor

with you

for I am here to be worshiped by those who embody the
presence to devour my sides

the hum and beat of my red ripe heart

do not come to the mountain

and refuse to feel her.

What if the great adventure
was rest.

SOMETIMES WE MUST RUN FROM THE HEAT OF THE CITY

we must run from the exhaust

the car horns

the traffic lights

the sound of televisions on the fourth floor

playing into the night

we must retreat to where the only light

comes from fireflies

the moon

the sunshine as it shines upon the ocean

the lake

we must return to where there are wildflowers to pick

cedar docks to lie on

stars to gaze at in silence

laughter and stones being thrown

dogs barking

wasps buzzing

we must return to the womb of the earth

for she listens best

she cradles deepest

she loves hardest

she forgives easiest

if you need me

this is where I'll be.

SPLINTERS & SAP

I pace to and fro
play with my axe in my woodshed
throw around uncut cedar rounds as big as my thigh
sweat, chop, stack
listen to the rain dripping from the prayer flags
whack
the knot grabs my axe
I edge it out and swing again
whack
the wood splits
I hold the axe loosely in my hand
turn my face to the sky
the smell of cedar
the heart of my heat
rises like warmth melted by rain
my hands are like born again virgins
I will need to reacquaint them with
splinters & sap.

I TOOK YOU OUT TODAY

your letters written with ink
your love poems
the flowers from my land you left on my windowsill
they have dried now
they are still beautiful

I remember coming home
to you whittling wood on these steps
flowers on the doorstep
every windowsill
the fire built
heart rocks and love ballads

I needed all of that
you took care of me
showed up so subtly and sweetly
opened me
each crevice
'til my heart beat at the rivers and the mountains
thank you

You no longer belong shoved back
in that drawer
out of my heart's eye
I want you out here
to breathe

I want all the love I've had and will have to breathe

the loves in my past to be in the sunlight

you cannot fail at love

we can only dance

and darling, how we danced

'til my feet stopped and all that remained was the thud of
my heart

I want to shout love from mountaintops

through this fog

what's the shame?

I loved you darling

we should celebrate the ones who carry a piece of our soul

even if they do not stay forever

I honor you

I cherish you

I am not blowing at the embers of our love

to start anew

you've opened to another

so have I

I hope she loves you with all her might

I hope you're full and thriving

I am simply saying

there ain't no one like you

your voice runs its fingers along the logs of my cabin this
morning

and I feel nothing but love for you.

Love less quick

she said

yes

love

less

quick

I'm sorry what was that?

I was too busy

loving.

You are in the milk of my coffee, the road beneath my feet, the yellow of the flowers that hang gently in the sunlight. You are in my blue cotton shirt that falls upon a woven grass chair as my hands pitter patter away as I write my grandfather an email.

You are here today.

IT'S 3 AM
I dress in black lace
Double Trouble plays
inside the red living room
trying to seduce love
with too many candles
for a man visiting at 3 AM
blue denim
loosely unbuttoned
whisky
no ice
good whisky
that bites
in a mason jar
I answer the door
it's snowing outside
I pull him inside
and he pretends to care
and I pretend not to
and we make love that is good
but without love
and he doesn't sleep over
and in the morning
I wish he had.

JUST BECAUSE YOU WISH TO LOVE A POET DOESN'T MEAN YOU SHOULD TRY TO BE ONE

I say I'm done

he writes

and writes

and writes

and writes

poems

poems

more poems

they're awful

just because you wish to love a poet

doesn't mean you should try to be one

more poems

oh God—stop

no more poems

one day

my prayers are answered

they stop

then

he writes me

"I deleted all our messages, will you send me the poems?"

I didn't write back

the poems shouldn't have been written in the first place.

DEAR MEN (II)

if you sleep with a woman

for fuck's sake

call her the next day

call her the next day if you work 20 hours

call her the next day if you have the flu and spent the night hugging the toilet bowl

call her the next day if your car breaks down and you spend 7 hours at the mechanic's

call her and tell her that her legs are the most beautiful walking sticks you've touched

call her and tell her being inside of her was like coming home

call her and tell her she shook the rocks to the mountains and that you've had the smell of her brown shoulder on your mind since breakfast

call her and beg to see her again

tell her if you don't

the sun will not rise

the stars will not shine

the ocean will cease to swell

the clocks will stop

call her and tell her all you can feel are her lips left on your neck

call her and say you have never felt a body that fit so sweetly in your arms

that you spent your entire day dreaming of being hip locked and drowned in her grey and blue eyes.

THIS IS ABOUT AN ITALIAN

You know how you can know I like you

how?

he asks

because I walk down and up this fucking hill for you

because I'm a grandma

and when I go up

I do not want to come down

I want to sit in my brown rocking chair

with Chopin

and drink tea

but I walk

in the moonlight

in the shadows

sweating and hot

for you.

But

I pull back

I have lice

or I had them

give them to me

he says

give them all to me

I'll take them

and he sticks his tongue deeply into my mouth

and his fingers inside of me

and I am lost as the world goes sideways and my fingers grasp your brown curls.

I'm hungry

what are you hungry for?

he asks

Latino?

he winks

no

I reply

I had that for breakfast.

ANOTHER POEM ABOUT HOW
I HATE SUBURBIA

It wouldn't be acceptable to turn to someone

and say

your life makes me absolutely miserable

to a world that doesn't think for themselves

that operates off societal shoulds

so I yell at it

all of them

with my pen

take big bites out of the mundane

spit it angrily

in the face of those who'll listen

I'm so sick of suburbia

of minivans

of house alarms

green grass that's watered every day at 4 PM

perfectly manicured lawns

brown loafers

a beige sitting chair

where one sits and reads The New Yorker

counts his money

his money bought this chair

his money bought this house

his money bought the china in the cupboards

you couldn't pay me any amount of money

to live in this house

cook this man dinner

do his dishes

clean his laundry

have boring missionary sex

wait 'til he kicks the clock

to begin to live.

I SHOUT AT THE STARS

why?

and the moon bellows down in all her fullness

you fucked up

and her sidekick the sun

who is usually smiling and yellow

peers over

and says

two men put their dicks inside of you

and now your heart gets to split in two

and I sink into the bathtub

in a deserving silence

and know there is nothing I can do.

I SWEAR SOME DAYS

in my rage with love

I transform

into a 30 foot troll

and I just want to pick up the men

as they run screaming away from me

with large stubby green hands as big as NYC office buildings

lifting them

screaming

towards my mouth as big as a semi truck

as I crunch their necks and bodies in between my teeth ruthlessly.

YOU'RE OPEN TO THE SERVICE AND
LEGS OF HEARTS EVERYWHERE

and it makes me so noxious I feel bile rise in my throat

insecurity and insanity grab the wheel

jealousy hops in with a cigarette dangling from the left side of her lip

blows the smoke of a Lucky Strike in my face

takes a swig of a Colt 45 and says

it's all true

he likes her

and he's going to fuck her

in that little red dress

before the night's through

my self-esteem sits quivering in the back of the bus

watching horrified

with a green lunch box that continues to jitter off the knees she has forgotten are worthy enough to stand

obsession is running up and down the road aisles of the bus saying, "It's true! It's true! He doesn't love you! He doesn't! It's true!"

and my nerves hum

and my heart screams

I am dropped to my knees by everything I am not and everything she may be to you

it's madness to throw away our power

strength and guidance are three buses back

and it's late and I'm not feeling beautiful or brilliant or desirable

I'm feeling not chosen

and alone

and the thought of another woman's hand in the small of your chest

as you sleep

in sticky September nights

shakes my spirit like a bull seeing red.

DESTINATION WEDDING

Since
"Destination wedding!"
is so original
you're going to Mexico?
no one does that
have fun at the feeding troughs
the bleached pools
beaches full of more gringos than sand
write "Cancun"
with your toes in the sand
go to the "shows"
that make me want to stab my eyes out with pens
girls half naked running around
onstage for the drunk slobbering imbeciles
but at least you're safe
in your artificially inseminated community
watching TV
in your air-conditioned rooms
eating hamburgers for lunch
desserts full of aspartame
and sugar—total shit
make sure to take a photograph
of the miserable crocodiles
in tiny pens

it's almost like 'Merica

y'all come back now, yah hear?

you want to read a funny poem?

put an isolationist in an all-inclusive resort

full of assholes in neon

I love Cancun

shirts and sombreros

I hate all of them

before you say

cheer up

remember that we all have a different version of hell.

KNOW THY TEACHER

People are so quick to dub themselves a leader

so quickly to attain sheep

who know little of the cause

the meaning

who are just so excited to be distracted from their lost lives

they cling to this thing

this person

for hope

for purpose

sometimes in doing so they incur harm

they alienate

ostracize

push others off the mental cliffs

drown in the ideals of another sheep

who's painted an enlightened crown on its head

foolishly

there are no crowns!

we are all down here

silly sheep

did you even stop to ask why?

is this for me?

do I believe this?

this goes for yoga

this goes for gurus

this goes for God

this goes for coaches

this goes for self-growth courses

stop and ask

why do I admire this person?

why do I kneel?

why do I pray?

know thy teacher

and only take what you need.

YOU KNOW WHAT SOUNDS GOOD
ABOUT MARRIAGE?

nothing

what is forever?

swearing to forever love

makes as much sense

as trying to photograph the stars

forever has as much use as the word perfect

we should throw perfect and forever

out the window

run over it a few times

tires on pavement

to and fro

yes, three times over

making a ring for realists

with the leftovers

make I do's

consisting of I'll love you like hell—for now, darling

for all we know is this moment

we do not know tomorrow

we invalidate yesterday

perhaps we are bored

pressured? guilty?

perhaps it is less we want to get married and more because
our parents want us to

I'm all for one love—monogamy isn't for suckers

it's delicate and tangible
it tastes like salt
feels like sunshine

Love is the grains of sand in our shoes we don't mind
the mini rocks that make life worth living
nah, love we must
love is the air for our souls' redemption
the answer, collectively to it all
both the why and the because

But must there be rings?
30,000 dollars' worth of petals?
such a fuss over fabric we wear once
and then it sits, collecting dust?
what for?
perhaps we should all get married naked
donate it instead to those who will hold the fabric to their
bodies and weep in gratitude
the minimalist in me vomits at the waste
extravagance
things, things, things
we are a society with such a hard-on for things
cannot love be simple?
as rolling in the long grass

at dusk

blue mountains in the sky

sleeping under the stars

drinking wine out of this morning's coffee cups?

Cannot love have weight, with just our words?

heard, here

by you and I's ears

must we gather all who we know,

so we all believe it

say, "Ah, yes"

have last names and a paper to prove it?

AGREEMENT ONE
is that while we take space
no talking

Agreement two
is that you can only write me
if you
in that space
realize you are walking towards me

Agreement three
if you
in that space
walk towards someone else
you tell me
because taking space
and letting go
are different things

Agreement four
if you have a certainty in your brain
and a clarity in your body
and you choose me
with confidence
walk towards me and find me.

IF YOU ARE TEXAS, I'LL STAY FOREVER

What is that?

the world sighs

desire

desire so loud that the maids came back

and shut the blinds

for we had sex in the roaring daylight

showing flesh and limbs to the world

and the prudes on the second floor

looked up

horrified

and called the front desk

Tanner answered

wasn't quite sure what to do

so when we got back

hot from riding a motorcycle in the musk of Austin on a Thursday night

the blinds were shut

silently

and we opened them

and had sex

again

and again

and the world below sighed

for they cannot taste the desire

they do not live

I have a fistful of your blond hair in my hand
your teeth on the purple flesh of my nipple
your body pulsing inside my thighs
and my moans call through the walls and into the night
and the bats shriek
and the cowboys walk in boots
that echo on sidewalks stained with love.

We are here for one day we stopped moving so wildly, only to land in a tornado of love so deep we make prayers each morning to never awaken to a life that is drained of the purple skies of our love.

If air is without you, I may live a hundred lives holding my breath. And if sleep is without you beside me, I will walk, red-eyed and tired 'til my body drops.

We have been completed for centuries—you do not fill any of my halves or corners for I am whole which is why each morning and each night I may rise to love you with the tenderness and strength you were born onto this earth deserving.

JANNE ROBINSON is a 21st-century feminist beat poet. Her voice haunts with the legacy of Charles Bukowski, Jack Kerouac and Gloria Steinem. Her no sugar shit prose cuts with the simplicity and honesty of Bukowski and the romantic reliability of Kerouac. Her poetry leads like a woman, walking with fire in the footprints of Steinem—breathing sexual liberation, choice, and overall championing women to their birthright of not only equality but of leadership.

She notoriously states that her career is to "share slabs of her heart for a living." Her ability to capture the human experience with unrefined sincerity makes her an incredible force in the modern landscape of personal expression.

Robinson's films and art shit on the societal "shoulds" and norms and encourage people to "build your own box." She is an outrageous idealist and master at effortlessly marrying the life she wishes to live with her work, and this enrages and inspires many who believe they are trapped.

Robinson's foray into directing and the multimedia world was in directing a spoken word poetry film in NYC involving 18 women reading the lines from her poem, "This Is For The Women Who Don't Give a Fuck." The film was a viral sensation online and was nominated for the 2016 Cannes Corporate Media & TV Awards.

Janne is very much so crowning at the beginning of what is and will be a triumphant career, and she has begun so with the hearts of millions indebted and watching, as it is rare to stumble upon a woman who makes revolution nature.

THOUGHT CATALOG Books

Thought Catalog Books is a publishing house owned by The Thought & Expression Company, an independent media group based in Brooklyn, NY. Founded in 2010, we are committed to facilitating thought and expression. We exist to help people become better communicators and listeners in order to engender a more exciting, attentive, and imaginative world. We are powered by Collective World, a community of creatives and writers from all over the globe.

Visit us on the web at *www.thoughtcatalogbooks.com* and *www.collective.world*.